In the Hands of the River

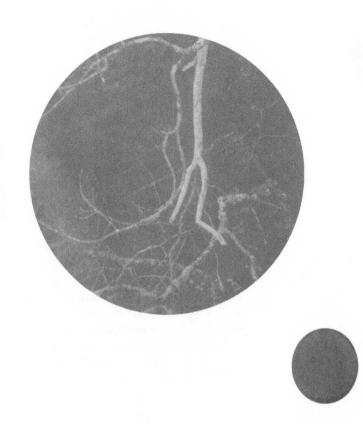

IN THE HANDS
OF THE RIVER

Lucien Darjeun Meadows

HUB CITY PRESS
SPARTANBURG, SC

Library of Congress
Cataloging-in-Publication Data

Meadows, Lucien Darjeun, author.
In the hands of the river / Lucien Darjeun
Meadows.
Description: Spartanburg, SC:
Hub City Press, [2022]
Identifiers: LCCN 2022019591 (print)
LCCN 2022019592 (ebook)
ISBN 9781938235993 (paperback)
ISBN 9798885740098 (ebook)
Subjects: LCGFT: Poetry.
Classification: LCC PS3613.E138 I5 2022 (print)
LCC PS3613.E138 (ebook)
DDC 811/.6—dc23/eng/20220427
LC record available at
https://lccn.loc.gov/2022019591
LC ebook record available at
https://lccn.loc.gov/2022019592

Hub City Press gratefully acknowledges support from the National Endowment for the Arts,
the Amazon Literary Partnership, South Arts, and the South Carolina Arts Commission.

HUB CITY PRESS
200 Ezell Street
Spartanburg, SC 29306
864.577.9349 | www.hubcity.org

TABLE OF CONTENTS

RUST

Out here, where wild gentians twist around rusted cars,
    These yards become indistinguishable—
        Porch swing, tomato patch, kiddie pool—

No matter if the kids have grown and gone—
    Some now far enough no neighbor can tell them
        The difference between lignite and anthracite,

Some just down the road, a pool of their own—
    No matter. Every plastic swimming pool turns
        From its original blue to rust pink in a year or two.

Down by the river's edge, we slip back to Biblical,
    See death as the ultimate baptism—whether lungs fill
        With the grit of a collapsing tunnel, riverwater,

Or both. Sometimes, beneath the moonlight, we lie down
    In our plastic pools to rest, to wait—if the rain fell right,
        This whole holler could be wiped clean in a night.

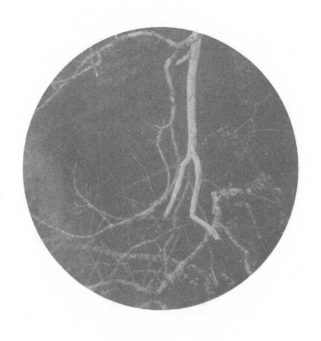

FIRST TIME
102 pounds

Not looking for oblivion, just silence
    On the roof of our old blue house that winter,
        Fields and mountains covered in snow,

Smoke on the horizon from the newest mine.
    Not thinking of the heavy thud, the ooze
        Of organs and blood, but the surrender

Into sky and air, the perfect nothing
    I, twenty pounds fewer now, long for.
        The sun falls behind the furthest hill

With a laugh, like a father walking out
    The front door, saying *See you tonight*
        And knowing *Never again, so help me god.*

        In the sudden twilight, I forget all
        I wanted, why I am balanced here.

♌

The screen door rattles, Sister shouting,
    Boo, where are you? And as she steps out
        On the porch, the slanted light pales her dress,

And I see her vertebrae like small smooth
    Stones jutting out from her back. I wait.
        Once she gives up, goes inside, I jump—

But not with the rope tied round the chimney
    As the letter under my pillow described,
        But onto a snowdrift, halfhearted and silent,

Not because of warm home, little sister,
    Absent father or god, but because
        Shivering up there, feeling the shake,

        Heft of stomach, of leg against jeans,
        I knew I could become smaller yet.

MONONGALIA COUNTY, WEST VIRGINIA

Red dirt never washes away—blue hills
Pocked by long grey scars from mines and slurry
Pools trembling, always, over someone's home,
Some holler's elementary school, green rivers,
Blue, brown rivers all running toward the old New,
Their deep gorge filled in autumn with so many
Red fingers pressed to the sky, like a revival,
Each candle lit by boys hoping to never be kissed.

Snowshoes out of dinner pails, that Appalachian frugality—
Making something out of nothing because
Our fathers took these mountains and turned into
Nothing. Coats filled with leaves, each stone a home
Cracked open. We are always searching for light
And finding a hoofprint, a heartbeat, the moment
A hill disappears and the tunnels of your blood
Vibrate a golden song just a little too late.

NIGHT/OˑRT (USVI)

Oil, acrylic, wax, and copper on canvas, Kay WalkingStick, 1991

even as a girl, her parents called her

little elf   pine cone
elisi   grandmother

running her hands down my back
she can predict the rain

wind through her trees   how many days
before my father will come home

child of wolf   my plum-eyed boy
atsutsa I lost   returns in you

stay inside when the moon wanes
there is silver, not coal   in your spine

keep it there, the moon is hungry

I close my windows   I still believe

BEFORE THE SIRENS, MY MOTHER OFFERS LIGHT

This morning, in the kitchen of my childhood,
　　My mother stands at the sink in a peach sundress,
　　　　Blonde hair long again and tied in a wide-eyed bow.

Her back to me, she pours water from a crystal vase
　　Through her fingers, light through the window
　　　　Scattering purple and gold across her arms.

Once, there was a father who sold his horses
　　So this girl could take the family name to college,
　　　　A girl who abandoned study to play nocturnes,

Who, when the record snowfall arrived, they found
　　By following husks of her clothes discarded over
　　　　Frozen ground, path ending at the chapel where

Bareskinned and feverish, days without food, she left
　　Nocturne for fugue: fingers unraveling chords
　　　　As they carried her away. How weeks pass,

How many months, snow trembling the corners
　　Of that soundless room. After, white crystals
　　　　In an alley, shiver of hands, her hungry face.

Once, there was a baby who broke open
　　His world with a cry for light and pure speed,
　　　　Born to a mother who forgot how to sing,

Body housing a small girl who watches for ice
　　And prays for rain, books piled beside her,
　　　　A restless child, eyes heavy with waiting.

Now, in the house we lost, my mother has poured
    Out all her water but stands caught in time:
        Hand open, arms like stained glass in the light.

Somewhere, her fugue begins. Her fingers move:
    Her light jumps onto my face. I cannot speak.
        I take off my ears and lay them at her feet.

TONGUE

Chickadee, Cherokee,
Talon, sadness, Tsalagi
The tongue curls into itself

Into roads reft with—what?
Telephone books, beech,
Sycamore the camouflage tree

And a boy made of shards
Warp and weft of Appalachia
Tin bucket ring of *wado wado*

To be red not brown to be
Red but passing white
In this winter-hollow holler

Ten thousand silenced stories
Under every tree, a home
For a tongue: our exchange.

HOLLER

Growing up, we lived down in a holler, and sometimes,
Coyote loped through our fields—nothing to eat but okra
And tomatoes—before crossing the dirt road to Baker's farm.
Sometimes, the scream of a chicken. Sometimes, gunshot,

Silence. When we moved in, neighbor Johnson spoke
Low to Father, *You got a gun? Here, you are your own police.*
Only trees will hear you holler. But when storms crashed through,
Father and I would cross treeline to stand fieldbare, breathing

Wet earth—my red toes reaching like roots into dirt,
His hair plastered over shoulders and back like wolfmane—
To howl and holler into lightning, voices thick with thunder

As we watch mountains close around us, push back olive sky,
Sacrifice some hilltop sycamore so only rain comes running
Down here: flashriver, summerflood, wash our holler out.

BECAUSE WE WANT HORSES

Everyone has come to the field today.
    Shirtless, Father leads the goat-neighbor's boys

In pacing out each post, *And you set it,*
    And you fill it with concrete. Men dig holes

As I slip my hands along wire coiled
    And waiting, imagine the arc of light—

Light I will touch, startling the horse
    Father and I share, light who will fill me

Years later in a cold room after I forget
    How to smile, eat, speak. Then I will see

December by my left shoulder,
    Summer somewhere behind, and know

The peach-pepper taste of blue.
    Father's voice a cascade of slurry

As smoke sharpens to copper and salt,
    Front door swinging loose behind him—

I drop the wire. I run to the hole
    My father walks toward, and I jump in,

These arms pressed rigid to my sides, straight
    As a post. How I hope for concrete.

He smells like pennies as he lifts me out,
    Swats me with a smile, says *Atsutsa, go play.*

DRAGONFLY

I steal your body from a clutch of blue lupines
    Wild by the stream beside my house. When I unfurl
        Four stained-glass wings—a fading gold like evening
Or autumn chrysanthemums, black-tipped—
    To lick dry pollen from your bristled legs, I see
        Your infinite eyes veiled with death's indifference,

And I swoon into my future corpse, my body
    Your body, here, splayed under unforgiving light.
        I detach your wings. Your exoskeleton offers
Only slight resistance. In my hands, you lie
        In pieces.

NO MORE THE COUNTING OF MARBLES

A black goat wheeling through fresh-planted sky,
    But Father saw me as a tangle of wind,
        A locust drone. *He must be watched,*

Mother said, so I left school for home, teacher
    For crow. My sister the magnolia tree
        Watched me sew leaves to skin, forget how

To sing except behind my mask of branches.
    You are no longer a child, she whispered
        As I dragged a bag of rocks to the river,

But I could not hear her above
    This bleating inside each hollow bone—

DESCENT

The Spring my father disappeared
Into the mines, he surrendered
His crowfeathers for the heavy coat

Of a wolf, falling into an open sky
Bound by cavern and tunnel, breath
And stillness. In late September,

The day his blue Ford finally returned
To our hollow, impenetrable night
Came with him, darkness folded

In his long hair, blackness buried
Under his fingernails. Memory of fire
And endless voices drowning in smoke.

Later that night, on my pillow I found
A piece of coal the size of a wolf's eye: lidless
And blind, cold moon locked into silence.

WHEN THERE IS NOTHING TO EAT

I am in the fridge again as Mother
Crushes the *not for you* into white roads
On her empty plate. These nights, home becomes

The constant threat of an electric chair,
Other mothers' faces pulled into screams.
Our TV plays the trials, nothing else.

I keep finding apple seeds in my hair.
I keep twisting wire from the old horse fence
Tighter around my wrists. I am grieving

My father—coal-crusted boots, the sickening
Lift when I run down the mountain too fast,
When I see a boy and think of kneeling.

In the living room, the nights' screams begin.
Here in the fridge, I lay my head beside
A black cabbage and bite my tongue until

It bleeds. I watch my blood fall on the shelves,
The weeks-old meat, dappling all red and white
Like the fox in snow Mother ran over

A few days ago. Bleeding in the road,
His hind-legs broken, he lifted his head
And brayed as she reversed the truck, ran him

Over again. Forward and back again,
Turning up the radio. Driving home,
She laughed—*Smile, there's nothing else we can do.*

RUBY IS HER BIRTHSTONE

Straightening the pile of books and bottles
    Beside your chair after I come home
In the evening, Mother, I find a ruby bracelet
    Under a notepad with your maiden name
Written over and over. I try it on.
    Your eyes open, seaglass and red cloud,
And you call me by my father's name,
    Fern of your hand curling whiteknuckled.
When I step behind your chair, your head
    Falls forward—

I am a child, and you are singing Evita
Through our house. I spend the July day
Dropping blackpocked rubies of beetles
Into our well as I whisper along,

       The truth is, I never left you.

You drive us an hour to see the show
In Morgantown, wearing this bracelet.
Wearing violets I gathered from our field
Pinned to your sundress by a dragonfly.

℧

Another July, I stumble inside to find Father
Holding you onto the toilet, nightgown twisted
Above your hips, hands opening and closing
Around his head like gills of suffocating fish.

I run—a bag of books and jelly sandwiches
And I climb the tallest hill in our hollow,
Lay down and wait for rain, to become
A quiver of foxglove, silent bells.

But I saw Father's suitcases, know he leaves
Tomorrow, so deerdreaming, still hearing
Your song, I run back down the mountain,
Jump home through my open window—

I watch you still, your mouth open.
    I unclasp the bracelet, put it around
Your wrist. Breathing loud, your body
    A brown honeysuckle left empty
In the sun after a boy pulls the sword
    Of long tongue from throat.

STRAWBERRY SEASON

Come harvest, come days of sixteen hours'
Light kneeling in the fields over each blush,

Each red burr, fingertips stained like spilled wine
And smelling somewhere between mimosa

And charcoal. Eight weeks falling through the year
In a day, a brief smile, nights of candles

And the bone-weariness of red dirt pressed
Deep enough to stay the coming winter.

How winter was a distant grandfather
Living up north, whose annual visit

With slate-grey eyes who stared us to silence,
Filling my stomach with acid and smoke,

Was never certain. He is just shadow
Compared to scent of berries and oakmoss

Here, now, sap rising like wax in our cups.
We had never seen the ocean, but we

Imagined how our bodies still felt
The kneel, pluck, rise beside the plants at night,

With salt on our lips instead of sugar
And the same delicious thrill of drowning.

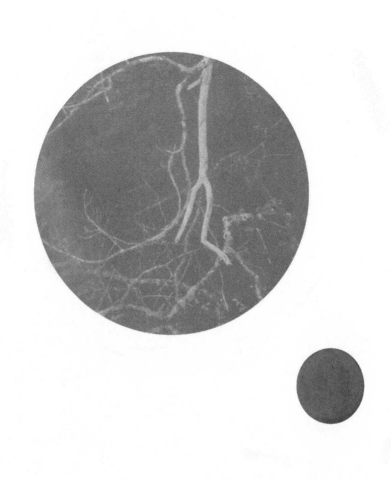

SECOND TIME
85 pounds

A boy with a knife and a hot bath drawn
At midnight is impetuous. At high noon

Is deliberate. He knows the sycamores
Shake their gold leaves at him, laughing.

He knows his mother will never wake up,
Not really, not to smile and dance

As she did when his father was here.
He knows his father is never coming back—

The crows told him so. They clatter loud
Through his arms when he tries to sleep,

A frenzy of claws and feathers and beaks
He can still only by cutting them free,

And today, everyone gets to fly home.

FIELD JOURNALS

By the treeline, a black plastic hardback
    With a melted clasp for a dime-store key.
One is of blue cloth, bought at a trade fair
    Down in Cherokee, North Carolina.
Another, palm-sized and the spine ridged
    Where all the pages were once pulled out.
Pages scatter the field like grey feathers,
    Words written in pen, in pencil, in blood.

I want to set these fields afire, to burn
    The last remains of my childhood down
Into the land and let it all grow back
    As the flowers I compared each boy to,
Or as the grass under it all, subtle
    As my father's smile and yet dangerous
As anything that clings to this red earth
    Waiting to be cut, blown into the sky.

CLOVER

Sunday morning, these white cedar walls
Multiply the tulip poplar leaves just outside.
I pray, sing, and try to mind the preacher—

Last night, I waited in my family's field,
On my back, shoeless, shirtless in clover.

You called me Crow. You said *Sometimes
Death would be easier than this,* and I said
Then come west with me—

But with ten generations of fathers
Mining and preaching behind you,
Holler is the only home you will ever know.

SEVENTEEN

The winter before I leave home, I start
    Running each afternoon while Mother sleeps,
Sister curled around her. *I will be back.*
    Entering the forest is like pushing
Off into sleep—my feet silent on moss,
    The cool air I dream a mother's embrace.
When I reach the top of our hill, when I
    Run down the south side between rocks and see

The horizon bald like a toothless mouth,
    Our neighbor's hills no longer there, I have
Pulled myself into the space between heart
    And rib, body my machine rocking me
Past hours as I run through falling white
    Feathers, clouds above plucking themselves bare.

AS TELEMACHOS

Clatter of your black clotheshangers swinging
Hungry as nooses in the hall closet, your tin cup

Tarnishing at our table's empty head—I remember

You, Agidoda, Father, through innumerable absences—
My footprints to your toolshed filling with rain

Like boats slowly sinking, the right side of her bed

Drawn tight as a dead man's smile. I hear your voice
A baritone of thunder when I go running: deep

In the forest, I pass through a pocket of sudden chill—

Each tooth in this bonesore mouth revolves
Slowly, in its socket. How bats wear your name

Across the candelabra of their wings, every syllable

A coalspark, a burning, then a smudge of ash. Inside,
I watch them circling. I splay fingers against window,

Dream the glass your face, akta I have never seen.

℘

She says you have these brown akta, black hair.
I want to believe this body is not an accident—

Hard to grow up amid blonde cornflowers
As some dark columbine. When you were a boy,

Did you also spend spring facedown in uweyv'i
Leaping toward the Kanawha, behind your home,

Turning skyward only when floating turned
To gadosga, and falling to a familiar darkness

That smelt of alfalfa and blood? Could you
Slip between fenceposts, fold yourself into

A dresser drawer? Did you uncap a marker
And find the tunnels of your father's mine

By connecting your freckles? Would you,
Then, take a knife and turn lines into scars

That silver the strange opposite of coalseams,
So, hearing night's vacuum of stars punctuated

Only by coyote, you could trace those ridges,
Imagine your father crawling through your skin?

ೲ

When I was fourteen, I went down to our river.

I filled my pockets with stones, then crossed
The field and threw myself into our empty well

Because I wanted to know what mining was like—

Walls began to breathe, oozing eyeless insects
That crept over me, slicking my skin, my feet

Sinking into a thick murk of slurry and I began

To scream, clawing this cage, ripping my nails—
It was the next day before she realized I was

Gone. Agidoda, how do you live without sunlight,

Dragging yourself deep through Earth's belly
Like a worm, seeing only vibration and heat?

ℰ

For months now, a cave wrenches a meadow
Apart between my feet. Each night I fall, gadosga,

Gadosga for hours. I am afraid of hitting bottom.
When I wake, my jaws hinge wide, gasping

Air that cuts my lungs like a straight razor
Into snow. My eyes open. I am kneeling

Bareskinned at the edge of our well, fingers
Mud-streaked, lips chapped open. Warmth

In agwoyeni: I hold bat wings. Sometimes
They bleed. Sometimes I do. Agidoda, I need

You to come home. I have only a picture
Of you, taken by her when you were my age,

But you are just a blurred shadow running
Under the mossy limbs of a willow. At dawn,

I will leave, that picture and a list of cousins
In my pocket, disappearing to search for you.

SHADOW

The animal of you running toward my mother

  As the front door falls from its hinge,
  Your fist punched through the screen—

The space between boy and man lengthening

  Into mountains to climb, hiding under
  Useless bushes, taste of blood and sugar

In the rain. Feet cracked raw from running down

  The last gold canary before the flood comes
  And your father's house buckles into the river—

I follow you by what you leave behind:

  A shout in the limbs of a grandfather pine.
  These white cotton fields, mud and ash.

The cellar where your father once locked you

  For a week without food to become a man,
  Till you cut your skin loose with a wolf's tooth—

LADY'S SLIPPER

Open field, never make a sound. What if
Our mothers could see us now. Your broad hands
Find delicate straps, blush of silver, gold.
Let me always fit in your palm. Let us
Always love right here, right here. This red land
Our blood, our death without resurrection.
But these nights—the stench of coal and oil lost
In your cinnamon body. My hands reach,
Fill with lace. The furthest place from daylight.
Click of buckshot, red flash, the chase. Always
Our fathers. Always the watching. Push your
Head lower, where petal lets down lip. What
Can we do but seek nectar where it blooms.

VIOLET

Cloud, birdfoot, common blue. Blush in your sex,
Bruise on my chin. Chalk dust and moth wings. Quiet
Under sycamore. My face pressed to bark.
Squish of toes in spring mud. Stillness after.
River rising beside, we hear the call—
More silence than whisper, smell of first rain
Never leaving my palms, tongue. We love like
No other blooming. Never trillium,
Angel's trumpet, beebalm. First spring wind, new
Fuzz on your chin. Slant of light, your long hair,
If only, only, to hold hands walking
Down the dirt road. Somewhere a deeper shade
Of blue. Backs of your knees cup like petals,
Filled with salt. These long nights of rain, what thirst.

CLEAVE

The summer everything changed, I walked out
Past the field, into the forest, toward the cleft
In the hill, on the darker side of the river.
Our entire house could fit into this swollen gap
No father or grandfather could explain.
Sitting on the edge, swinging my feet, I leaned back
And fell, wrist-deep, into the body of a deer,
Just a fawn, really, with no eyes. His mouth was open,
His tongue black, swollen, vibrating with flies.
My hand in his stomach, I looked up, up, past
The sycamores, toward the sun, clotted by cloud.
I did not do this. But my hand was inside him,
And only the rustling of darkness over the trees
Brought me to my feet.

SING OUT

Cleaning the house each morning, Elisi
Sang along with Simon & Garfunkel,
Smoke-rough alto just a different shade

Of countertenor. Sweeping the coal dust
From the house in her paisley skirt,
I am just a poor boy echoing

As I walked across the holler to school.
One night, after Eduda was asleep,
Elisi told me she ran off to New York City

As a girl—rode the bus to Charleston,
Then Baltimore, then Philadelphia,
Up further than any family had been,

Carrying a banana and three packs
Of cigarettes in her purse. I should have
Listened closer. This year, after her burial

I found her cabinets empty but her freezer
Filled with books, and a scribbled bird
On a napkin, *To Lin: Sing Out, Love Art.*

THIRST

Tonight, I follow the song to the river,
Brown water thick with falling brown leaves.
With a breeze, the river vibrates and breaks
Like a great wing, or a door punctuated with light.
Without wind, without you, the river hollows
Like the thigh bone I once saw a wolf suck dry.
I do not believe this thirst will ever be filled.
And still the song, a grackle or a crow—
All songs become eulogies in November.

Somehow I am standing in the water, now,
And leaves clap my legs like cold hands,
Your hands the last time we met, just upstream,
When I reached for your belt, and you
Hit my face, held it, hit it again as you said
I have never, never known you. I fell to my knees.
You left, and I am still falling, here, and if
I fell forward, I would fall through this river,
This song. But the night is too short. It always is.

PRELUDE

Sister, you fidget your mashed potatoes
Across your plate, fingers blue at the tips.
My hands ladle potatoes, gravy, *to be*
A good example. Your shoulders vibrate.
I know your legs churn the butter of air
Under the table. Mine itch. I take a bite.
You raise your hand to spill ketchup: bright gash,
A hemorrhage down potato canals—

One year older than you when I learned *cut*
Vertical, not horizontal and brought
The blade down my right arm, snapping the vein
Like harpstring—flesh pulling apart like dough.
Inside, packed styrofoam potatoes of fat—
I wanted a spoon to scoop down to bone.

POND

Today, Sister, we could be anywhere.
   The leaves on the willows around us fall
      On the cold skin of this pond. When you stand,
   You sway, closing your eyes. As you sink down
      On the sharp grass, you say that Mother found

Your stash, steak knives, would not stop shouting
   Until you showed your thighs, pink serrated
      Lines evenly spaced, fading to grey. You say
   She made an appointment for you where I
      Went one day and did not leave for four years.

I push my hands into the teeth of this
   Parched grass, wanting to feel blood. Your blue eyes
      Unfocus, breath scattered as the willow
   Branches touching the water, leaning back—
      Then, with the breeze, going under, to sleep.

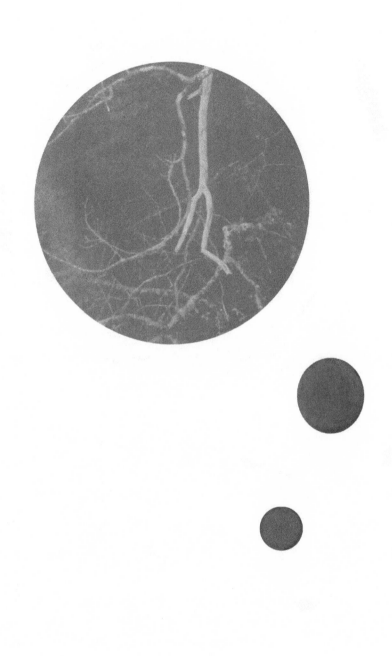

THIRD TIME
70 pounds

You said it would be easy as slipping.
Into a warm bath. As falling asleep.
To the rocking of my father's truck down.
The holler, the only thing that made me.
Stop crying as a baby. You said not.
Eating would help. Me or them, you never.
Said. Me or you. I never knew you would.
Use your father's gun. My hands only knew.
The painkillers in our mothers' cabinets.
To take you to the edge of the river.
That last night. You said it would be a dream.
In technicolor to never forget.
Not that we would care. You never said I.
Would wake days later in the well, my note.
Unread on my pillow. You never said.
I would find you. Never said your body.
Could hold that much blood.

EIGHTEEN

There is no soda pop, no pool party, no camping trip,
    No ice cream. No stadium seats, no t-shirts,
No dreamless sleep. Only the threat of losing another
    Year to hospital beds and the hot blue electric.
Dress in the softest cotton, now, dress in scars

    Because blood seems softer than air, and you
        Count the vertebrae, compare the hard nub
    Behind your neck to an acorn, Adam's apple.

Keep your hair in soft cat piles in the corners
    Of your room, clip it every other week
So the shower drain does not clog, yet again,
    Sending you to the doctor, yet again.
Notice the breeze—how easily you are wracked

    With chattering teeth. Find a sliver of moonlight
        Between your thighs, then a triangle, then find
    Space between your calves, fingers, eyes—

Sometimes, it takes going deeper than blood, down
    To the white pillows of fat to realize this is you.
Use your father's knife, the vacancy in your mother's eyes,
    The river you both know took him and is coming
One of these days to set you some kind of free.

GLASS FOREST

In the glass forest, she knows the color
Of cold. Light like a broken clock, all springs
And hands across her back as she kneels, lifts

The only thing she knows is pure, anymore—
Winter trees cough a stream of black crows

Into the sky. She kneels in the snow to forget,
To be a girl without scarred arms, lips raw
From wire and ash. I follow her into

This forest, rub salt and ice into our skin,
Take the quick breath to forget, to forget.

Mother, you cannot hear me, but I also want
To tear loose every soft and hidden part
Touched as I slept, as a sister watched—

And I would scrape the carbon from my bones
To leave you barren, lungs filling with snow.

TWO MAGNOLIA BLOSSOMS
IN A GLASS VASE

Oil on canvas, Martin Johnson Heade, c. 1890

Beyond these locked windows, a world
    Of wind and birdsong. We could forget
        How cardinals splash snowfields red,
                A world
Where we would stand outside in winter,
        Eyes closed: we survived on swallowed light.
                A world
Of wind and birdsong we could forget.
Beyond these locked windows.

Your baby teeth,
Like wooden beads I string
On a gold thread to pass the hours.
My sister, you cannot grow
Always smaller. Now your arms
Curl like white ribbon in a fire.
Your eyes, edged in red.
Sister, do you remember when
We ran into the sky
Climbing our winter mountain
And the hollow was, below,
A bowl filled with milk?
In your snowsuit, your hands
Made of glass, of wind.
Here, I watch snow fall:
There is no mountain, no
Mother, no father. Brother
Sounding ever more like
Sunder. I am waiting for you, night
Sounding ever more like
Mother, no father, brother.
There is no mountain, no
Here. I watch snow fall
Made of glass, of wind
In your snowsuit. Your hands
A bowl filled with milk,
And the hollow was, below,
Climbing our winter mountain.
We ran into the sky,
Sister, do you remember when?

Your eyes, edged in red,
Curl like white ribbon in a fire.
Always smaller now, your arms.
My sister, you cannot grow
On a gold thread. To pass the hours
Like wooden beads, I string
Your baby teeth.

BIRTHDAY IS A TIME FOR BURNING

Open and uncurtained, my aunt's new windows
Face the field that leads to Elisi's house.

At night, my aunt wakes every other hour, sometimes
Already by the windows, watching. *I never know*

If Mom's house will still be standing. Across the field
Of overgrown clover and onion grass,

Elisi is sleepwalking again. Last week,
She made a two-tier cake for my aunt's birthday—

Red velvet and buttercream, forty white candles—
But in the night, she lit the candles, put the cake

Back in the oven, turned it to broil. *The smell,*
The smell. She woke from a dream of July bonfires,

Gas oven aflame, screaming—my aunt heard,
Grabbed her fire extinguisher ready by the door,

Ran down. *She will never surrender that house.*
A hot wind rattles pine needles over the porch,

Where we sit, brittle clumps. They fan
Over our feet in patterns, spiral of candles.

Just before daybreak, I walk past families
    Under blankets to the snack cab. Behind the counter,
Danishes fog their plastic bags, breathing.
    A bearded man smiles, gives me change—three quarters
That show where this train is heading. Today:
    The Kanawha to the New and the New River Gorge Bridge.
I trace the arch on a coin, find a seat alone
    At a booth for four. Dawn through the east windows, gold

Over these hands that have never seemed less
    Like my father's. If he were here, I imagine he would talk
About the times he and his cousins rafted the New,
    Finding abandoned coal camps, digging with their hands
For scrip older than their own fathers kept
    In gun cases. A boy says *Last summer my buddies and I*
Rafted Gauley to the New, nearly broke our necks.
    The bearded man says *Is that right? Where you from?*

The room shivers blue when the man says
    Buckhannon, my father's childhood home, and the boy
Mon County, my own—I close my eyes to smell
    The ginseng of field and holler but taste only recycled air
And coffee. We are close now. The boy
    Pushes his face against a window to see the Bridge—
Not yet, she'll be on the right, says the man,
    And I already know, am already waiting. I hold my coffee

And remember my father's callused hands
    I held nine years ago, our last Bridge Day. How I lost all
Pictures of him but one, taken from a distance,
    And I cannot remember his face anymore, but I see him
As a shadow, the arch of my bones,
    That man nodding to the boy but staring right at me,
That blue and gold flag pinned to the Bridge
    Above, that beckoning fall to brown water below.

BARE GRAPE VINE

Pen and ink on paper, Arthur Josephson, 1963

Hands thread through Ma Pearl's forgotten grapevines,
    thick stems wrapped around the growing trellis—
        I slip fingers between vine and iron,
    wait hours to feel the squeeze—lift my face
        to clusters of fruit, a blue almost black,
each thumb-sized and filling my mouth—sometimes,
    with teeth I peel skin from stem to expose
        flesh—August heat makes them quiver and sweat
a bead of violet I let fall upon
        my lips, let slide over my chin, my chest—
before clipping fruit from stem, tongue swimming
    in dark sugar—I am always
        barefoot—I never return home until
    the bats begin circling overhead—

ROSA LAEVIGATA

Elisi always said that out there, past
The sycamores and past the pines, somewhere
Up the mountain, was a white rose planted
By her last free ancestor, when she came
Down from the highest Appalachians.
When you find it, you'll smell it before anything—
Like butter and honey and the first day of spring.

Growing up in red dirt and brown water,
Belief in God fell short of in that flower,
Just round the corner—just up the next hill.
So many dreams, feet dangling the river,
Of sliding between cream-colored petals
Better than the softest sheets, falling asleep
Not to machines but the silver unbloom
Closing around this dark body, secret
Somewhere in these hills, in the underbrush.

EVENING PRIMROSE

Tonight, his back a granite cliff buffeted
By valley, his hands the rope pulling me

Toward the stars. Again, again, all diamond
Night our slow resurrection. Each coyote

Echo a baptism, distance between
This mountain and tomorrow further than

North from now, from south to hallelujah.
Under the wolf moon, we move like a cloud

Of pollen, a white cotton sheet billowed
Into sky. What legs are his, what hands mine.

LIKE SON

Brown eyes that leak the wings of crows,
There was a boy in your father's stride

That he once thought was you, that he said
You will never become. *Soft hands, watch him run.*

So open the front door with those hands
Blackened by summers rubbing his coal

Over your body, hands that know a boy feels
Like a nectarine, skin a sheer line between *hush*

And *never was.* Up from the treeline, a wind
Rushes featherthick, a fist. Your shoulderblades

Harden—step out and run. When you forget
You have feet, you will be free.

FENCE

The two-stall leanto built forty years ago,
The wooden fence posts set in concrete—

Splintering, all, under the men in hard hats,
With their clipboards and metal machines.
Somewhere, Elisi still lies cooling
Under a bed of yellow roses. Somewhere,

The brindle dog who died last week is still
Wrapped in a blanket, waiting for the ground

To thaw. This blue ridge has never seemed
So indistinct, so far away. Down in the forest,
Deer tear loose strips of bark and feed as snow
Thickens in the furred curtains of their ears,

Muffling all sounds into a distant heartbeat.
The backhoe groans, white snow to red, red earth.

If only she had lived forever. If only we had
Stayed, here, hands in red dirt and eyes bent
To each small growing thing instead of wondering
What was just over that Monongahela ridge.

OLD PORCH

Generations of fathers have sat here,
Outside the only market in this town

Too small for its own post office, watching
The mountains migrate across the holler.

How the furred slope is shaved bare, and the wind
Blows colder that winter, colder next spring

When that razor returns, slicing lower,
Past the skin of soil, down to the wet seams.

And the mountains fall and never come back
Like so many fathers in this coal town,

Empty as the train cars racketing past,
Shuttered houses of each year's newlyweds,

The men rocking their bones on this old porch,
Mouths opening and closing without sound.

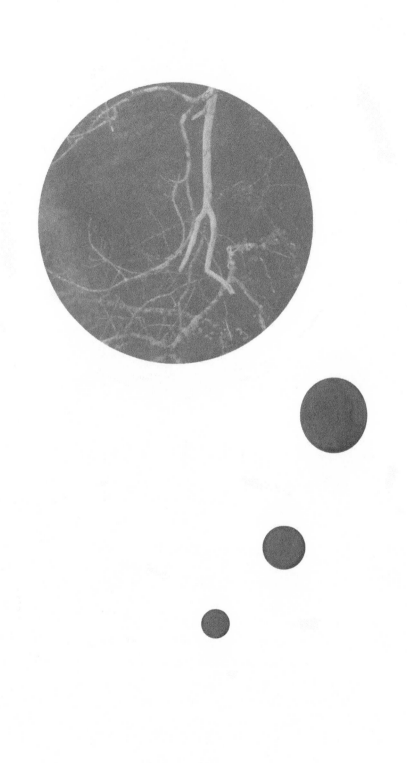

AFTER

What if the last pound possible to lose
            Falls away not as hollowed cheeks, but as
A flourish of fur on the backs of your
            Arms. Not as black hair but as sharpened teeth
Like the wolf your father. Not as the black
            Crow beating wings into a pulp of blood
And cartilage, but like the crow shocked blue
            You were last month in the hospital. You
Thanked god electricity has no weight.
            What is a boy. What is a boy kneeling
With his mouth open. Found by his father.
            Another boy's hands in his hair. What is
A boy in a dress but a laugh gone flat,
            A joke without a punchline. The hunger
Of a mouth for the river for the mouth.
            What if everywhere he touched you became
Invisible. Does weight exist if it
            Cannot be seen? And when he opened not
For you, but for the gun—though on his knees
            He called you *my derringer* and you loved
It—the last time he opened his mouth, wrapped
            His lips around a need—blood and brain wet
On his bedroom walls, the metallic clot
            Behind your throat for weeks, what is the weight
Of his laugh now. What bones did his mother
            Throw into the river. If you pull back
Your skin, dig past blood, fat, muscle to bone,
            Will he be there still, laughing his laugh that
You said always sounded more like a howl.

NIGHT IN THE BURNED HOUSE

In my old bedroom, in this house
Now my aunt's, walls mottle grey

Into black, char hiding that this room
Was ever painted purple in a hope

That someone *would guess*, would know.
Burning night, my hidden journals

Blown across the field—and my aunt,
Gathering boughs for wreaths, found

I love him. I have not seen her eyes
Since. She who sang hymns with me

As we hung the wash, who said
You can tell the Lord anything, and me too—

David and Jonathan a holy story,
But my love *a wickedness.* All night,

I press hands to these walls, whisper
What I cannot say without a flower

Opening, a disappearing boy, a house
Burning. Let the morning never come.

SOME MEMORY OF WRITING THE LAND

Summer mornings, Father's footsteps a steady meter
Across the field, each boot stirring red dust
Swung by the wind back to me with his scent,
An open parenthesis of ginseng and smoke.
Counting out his harvest—quatrain of okra,
A whole sestina of zucchini— and I mirror
Back to him: tadpoles in a bucket, tails splitting
Into legs, a line of sunflowers now shoulderhigh.
One May, mining a seam kept him away for weeks.
I found his notebook in the shed, almanac
Of weather and crop. With his drafting pencil,
I punctuated temperature reports, corrected each
Misspelling in blocky print. When he returned,
He barred me from shed and garden, so I sit
On the back porch, as I pick seeds from the face
Of a sun, cleave each iamb of shell: the taste—
Our language mixed with salt, these soft kernels
I gather, I pour into his hands each night.

SHENANDOAH

when he found you   no   you found
      him   on the mountain   and you sang
    he led you down   through the tunnels

tell me   when you first   knew
      to be   is to be for another

    tell me   he wears   your baby teeth
in the knob of his throat   and your knees
      are the moons   of his subterranean sky

    tell me   he would   hollow his bones
      to keep you   until you dissolve   into stars

STILL

Each time the phone rings I imagine
It will be Father on break from some job
Or traveling to one in the blue truck
That seems as much a part of him
As his long hair or faded jeans

And I will say *Hi Agidoda how's it going*
And in a voice I barely remember he will say
Working the mines in Mon County again
Where the mountains gave me your name

One of us sits alone at night picking
Mountains out from under his fingernails
And one of us remembers walking all day
To the highest peak in the holler
And both of us have found our eyes
In the hands of the river
And brought them home again for awhile

And I will say without saying *I stand*
In front of the mirror each night Agidoda
Searching for you in my own face
Because I am almost the age you were when—

Quiet for a minute then he will say
Something about how trees keep standing
Because they know when to bend
Or something about how the New River
We almost jumped into all those years ago
Is the oldest in America and *hey Bridge Day*
Is next month so nihi want to go with me

And I will say something about how
I still dream of him trapped in a mine
Because that was the only reason
I could imagine why he would disappear
And these fall days are getting shorter
But *you know* I can still remember spring
Which means *yes Father yes Agidoda yes.*

WRITING APPALACHIA

Light is just a promise at the end
Of the last day of winter, unspooling

Into the strands of electric light now
Strapped to my head, barbed and white-hot

As I shake against the hands holding me
Down, forcing me out of my childhood,

Out of the well, out of the home now burnt,
Out of my father stepping into his truck

As I come running up from the field, cutting
My feet on gravel as he drives away

To the mines and out of my mouth a slurry
Thick with a grit no one but me can see—

LANDSCAPE FROM A DREAM (RED OCHRE)

Acrylic on canvas, Christie Belcourt, 2008

Brown air clots with the fire in the mountain,
The mine burning and coughing a thick paste
Into the sky. Beside me on the porch,

Mother falls forward again, spilling her wine
On her yellow dress, jerks awake, demands
A towel, a drink, painkillers, her husband.

All afternoon, I have scratched a tally on my arm
With a safety pin of the times she stopped
Breathing, just for a moment—23—

And each gasp echoes my own when the skin
Opens and hot air rushes in, stinging
But dulling too soon. There is no TV

Or radio, since she pawned them last week.
No point in evacuation, nowhere
To go as black clumps of ash and grit fall,

The dogs running confused along the fence.
The holler echoes the shouts of the men
Down at the mine as our porch door swings, swings.

I lift the safety pin to my wrist, press
Down gently as I watch my skin tighten
(We are all alone here in this brown cloud)

And give way—she jerks awake again, then
Falls back asleep as a drop of blood beads
On my wrist, then falls into the red dirt.

FINDING HOME BY TASTE, BY FIRE

Monongalia mountains rub their shoulders blue
With horizon, these hills dreaming themselves sky.
Hardwood forest by the highway, woodblanket

For hills bared on the other side. I descend
From ridge to hollow, feel his coal in my pocket

Shake off the matte, oil itself glossy, hot—my leg
Glows red as the spray of cardinal flowers
Goat-high on a furred stalk, exhaling scarlet:

I breathe them in, set loose a flight of bees
From each pore of my face, who wing back

To drink each bright bell. As the trail rises again,
My ears vibrate with the drone of mosquitoes,
Machinery—a hum that still tells my body

It is summer, and tsadoda may never come home.

TO GRANDMOTHER'S BODY

Of water. Kanawha brown, Monongahela blue,
The Cheat and the New. Saying their names,
Hands rubbing together, hillbilly incantation.

Of Sundays and the September revival. The snakes
Smoothing your skin the one weekend a year
You could dance. Praise Jesus. Praise the old land.

Of knees rubbed with red dirt. The man
You never saw. Knife to your belly. The neighbor
Calling his dog, finding you still there, still shaking.

Of the man you loved like the river.
Of your daughters. Of the boy smudged
With crows. Of years edged in coal and salt.

The long last winter. A field of white moths,
The day you left. Of roses. Of darker
Roses. Bells in the distance, coming close.

FLITTERMICE

Now no deer will graze
        These fields. But when flittermice
                Spun from silk and leather

        Kite into sky, each star
                Seems not presence of light

But night's forgetting her station
        To flame a white blaze
                Through, from where sky is

        Synonym for wing and night
                A bright cup for dreaming.

From unshingled roof, one bat
        Hangs, their moonface a memory
                Of last winter's burning. Rafters

        To ash, and burst windows
                Become a glittering mosaic

Grouted in snow. Past horsefence,
        Three oaks have fallen, pocked
                With mushrooms, sweet rot thread

        Through this wind opening each
                Body of bat, tree, man,

Like a dandelion ghost growing
        Into fullness satisfied only when
                Loosed from body across land.

BUFFALO CREEK

Give us clover for remembrance, alfalfa
For thought, oniongrass to hide where
Where once was mountain, now dust—

When three earthen dams could no longer
Hold back the slurry our fathers carved

From the belly of these hills. Each Spring,
A prayer for grass to cover this pocked grave.
Not here but west, new fathers and cousins

Go to trust in other mountains. Never say
We never learn. We still give our bodies

Back to the land, as we force the land
To give their body to us. Mouths open,
We are the hollow their coalsludge now fills.

PORTRAIT OF MY FATHER AS ICARUS

My father climbs high branches above me
While on the grass, I hold sycamore leaves

To my face—I am a caterpillar
Burrowing tiny-eyed into a wall

Of green. I face the sun, one leaf over
My eyes revealing veins, and closer, skin

Patched like quilts. Skin into cell, and I see
Small boats of light canaling into leaf

Interrupted with a shout—my father
Falling from clouds like a god, knotted ropes

His slippery wings. Arms outstretched, his eyes
Open and silent as I run to him,

Smell mint and butter of sky in his hair.
Until he moves, we stay awhile like this.

IRONWEED

Mountain falling
Behind brown

Cloud who speaks in
Dry wind and smoke

Appalachian alchemy:

Riverstones grind
Brittle enough to turn

All coalshine into bone:
The diminishing is useful

Is forgetting

Is unstoppable as ironweed
Spiraling every fencepost

Into no analogy
But the land repeating:

Stay put.

WINTER SOLSTICE

after three weeks of snow   even morning folds
this hollow between mountains   in lengthening shadow
but when you follow me   back to our snowquilted bed
the yew beside us   bends a furred branch
to our window   lowers a cardinal
who spreads an exaltation of red   feather and wing

as we fall into thick drifts   each olive cone
swings on yewstem   when the cardinal trills
as if today   day of most darkness
each cone could disclose   nested red lips
these latent arils   open seedcups
a multitude of mouths   tongues tumbling toward river

and the cardinal tilts head   flutter and wing
yew branch waves   a beacon
a flame as I follow   the bright limbs of you
spiral through cloud and snow   out from our center
our horizon beginning   even now
to remember   the thrill of light

NOTES

Thank you to the journals and anthologies in which these poems initially appeared, sometimes with different titles and/or in earlier versions.

Appalachian Journal: "Some Memory of Writing the Land"
Appalachian Review: "Holler" & "Night in the Burned House"
Assaracus: "Field Journals" & "Ruby is Her Birthstone"
Barrow Street: "Because We Want Horses"
Beloit Poetry Journal: "Rust"
The Chattahoochee Review: "After"
Cheat River Review: "Birthday is a Time for Burning"
Ecotone: "Bare Grape Vine" & "Violet"
Hayden's Ferry Review: "Descent"
The Hopper: "Portrait of My Father as Icarus"
The Journal: "First Time"
Narrative: "Cleave" & "Third Time"
Nimrod International Journal: "Seventeen"
Passages North: "Dragonfly" & "Night/OʻRT (Usvi)"
Plath Profiles: "Before the Sirens, My Mother Offers Light"
Pleiades: "Glass Forest" & "Visiting My Sister in the Adolescent Ward"
Prairie Schooner: "Second Time"
Rappahannock Review: "Strawberry Season"
Shenandoah: "Monongalia County, West Virginia" &
    "To Grandmother's Body"
Still: "Evening Primrose," "Lady's Slipper," "Like Son,"
    "No More the Counting of Marbles," & "Writing Appalachia"
storySouth: "Still"
Third Coast: "Flittermice"
Two Peach: "When There is Nothing to Eat"
West Branch: "Prelude"
you are here: "Clover," "Shenandoah," "Thirst," & "Two Magnolia Blossoms
    in a Glass Vase"

"Descent" was selected by Iris Jamahl Dunkle for an AWP Intro Journals Award, 2014.

"Night in the Burned House" was nominated by *Appalachian Heritage* for a Pushcart Prize, 2015.

"As Telemachos" was a finalist for the *Fairy Tale Review* Poetry Prize, 2016.

"Bare Grape Vine" was nominated by *Ecotone* for Best New Poets, 2016.

"Finding Home by Taste, by Fire" was printed in *The World is Charged: Poetic Engagements with Gerard Manley Hopkins*, eds. William Wright and Daniel Westover (Clemson University Press, 2016).

"Rust" was reprinted and featured on *Poetry Daily*, 2017.

"On the Train, I Wake in West Virginia" and "Rosa laevigata" were printed in *Anthology of Appalachian Writers*, ed. S.L. Shurbutt (Shepherd University Press, 2017).

"Portrait of My Father as Icarus" was nominated by *The Hopper* for Best of the Net, 2018.

ACKNOWLEDGMENTS

This *River* is a confluence of many streams of reading and inspiration. I am grateful to the following writers, some of whom I know only through their printed words, whose cadences have inspired and might surface in this collection:

Marilou Awiakta, Billy-Ray Belcourt, Kristin Bock, Traci Brimhall, Lucie Brock-Broido, John Clare, Henri Cole, Eduardo C. Corral, Qwo-Li Driskill, Jennifer Elise Foerster, Thomas Hardy, Chloe Honum, Gerard Manley Hopkins, Thomas James, Saeed Jones, Jesse Lee Kercheval, Janet McAdams, Davis McCombs, Irene McKinney, Sandra Meek, Tyler Mills, Simone Muench, Astrida Neimanis, Sylvia Plath, Lee Ann Roripaugh, Richard Siken, Kathleen Stewart, Diane Thiel, and Anna Lowenhaupt Tsing.

Several poems in this collection are direct descendants, often in form, of other writers' work. I acknowledge my particular debt and gratitude to the following writers for these headwater poems and for their additional influence across this *River*:

Karen An-Hwei Lee's "Hyacinth Sea Room" ("Visiting My Sister in the Adolescent Ward"), Joan Naviyuk Kane's "Epithalamia" ("Tongue"), Mari L'Esperance's "To Her Body" ("To Grandmother's Body"), Dave Lucas's "To Say Nothing" ("Strawberry Season"), Michael Minicucci's "Lamentations" ("Violet"), and Jacques J. Rancourt's "Black Horse" ("No More the Counting of Marbles") and "The Wake" ("Third Time").

This book would not exist without the advice and support of mentors at critical moments. Rick Pringle, for hosting all-afternoon thesis meetings, introducing me to ethnography, and playing the believing game. Elizabeth Spires, for encouraging me toward graduate school and patiently mentoring this first-generation student throughout the process and after. Allison Joseph, for helping me continue writing amid highly challenging circumstances. Camille Dungy, for bringing me back into voice and poetry. Joanna Howard, for showing me how to read, make, and hold space in the work and in the world. Eleanor McNees, for modeling a life of continual learning as a luminous teacher and scholar. Dear mentors, I am so grateful to you.

Thank you to the organizations who supported what would become this River. Kratz Center for Creative Writing, for sending me to Europe, where I gained the distance to realize I most wanted to write about the hills and hollers of home. Bread Loaf Writers' Conferences, with particular gratitude to Noreen Cargill, Jennifer Grotz, and Jason Lamb, for welcoming me to those gorgeous green hills for transformative shelter, community, and inspiration. Colorado Creative Industries, for giving me back in Appalachia to revise several of these poems. The American Shakespeare Center in Virginia, for an unforgettable week of performances among the hills.

Thank you also to the professors, workshop leaders, and guides who inspired me on this *River's* journey, with special thanks to John Elder, Ross Gay, Sean Hill, Robin Wall Kimmerer, and Emily Wilson; Jeffrey Myers and Arnie Sanders; and Patrick Cottrell, Rachel Feder, Bin Ramke, Selah Saterstrom, and Lindsay Turner. I am particularly grateful to Carol Allen, librarian extraordinaire and lover of poetry.

Thank you to the colleagues and friends who, in various ways, have encouraged this manuscript into being. Laura Ruffino and Seanse Ducken, for fried pickles, one-hundred-mile drives, and pages of handwritten notes. Sara Sheiner and Alison Turner, for helping me find confidence in the work and room at the table. Ben Caldwell and Bailey Pittenger, for always being willing to talk Appalachian hollers here two thousand miles from home.

Thank you to the organizations and individuals, mentors and friends, who practice and advocate for inclusive environmental and place-based writing. I am particularly grateful to Jenna Gersie and the editorial team of *The Hopper.*

Thank you to George Brosi, Lisa Kwong, R.T. Smith, Laura-Gray Street, Lesley Wheeler, William Kelley Woolfitt, Marianne Worthington, and many, many others, for supporting these poems and being dynamic advocates for and voices of Appalachian writing.

Thank you to the talented writers and translators with whom I've been honored to share space in conference communities. Special thanks to David DeGusta, Joy Landeira, Michelle Whittaker, and my writing group for the 2021 Indigenous Literary Studies Association Gathering.

Thank you to the amazing team at Hub City Press for their warm support of this *River*. In particular, thank you to Meg Reid for welcoming me to the Hub City community. Kate McMullen, for taking these pages and creating a gorgeous book with the support of Jeannie Hutchins and her incredible art. Katherine Webb, for such generous gifts of time, patience, and expertise. Kate and Katherine, your intuitive ordering makes this *River* flow. Meg, Kate, and Katherine, you are the best editor-aunties I ever could imagine.

Thank you, always, to the Eastern Band of Cherokee Indians, and to the Cherokee Nation and the Cherokee Nation Language Department.

Thank you to the river, the hills, and the holler who raised me and who I still see as I fall asleep.

This book is dedicated to the memory of my grandmother, without whom none of this would be.

Deepest gratitude to my mother and father.

Thank you, also, to relatives near and far, born and chosen. Thank you to the ancestors who have gone before and who are still to come.

And Bobby, my partner, beloved, magical poet and musician and thinker—every winter solstice, every flower, everything and all of me, always for you.

PUBLISHING
New & Extraordinary
VOICES FROM THE
AMERICAN SOUTH

HUB CITY PRESS is a non-profit independent press in Spartanburg, SC that publishes well-crafted, high-quality works by new and established authors, with an emphasis on the Southern experience. We are committed to high-caliber novels, short stories, poetry, plays, memoir, and works emphasizing regional culture and history. We are particularly interested in books with a strong sense of place.

Hub City Press is an imprint of the non-profit Hub City Writers Project, founded in 1995 to foster a sense of community through the literary arts. Our metaphor of organization purposely looks backward to the nineteenth century when Spartanburg was known as the "hub city," a place where railroads converged and departed.

RECENT HUB CITY PRESS POETRY

Thresh & Hold • Marlanda Dekine

Reparations Now! • Ashley M. Jones

Sparrow Envy: A Field Guide to Birds and Lesser Beasts • J. Drew Lanham

Cleave • Tiana Nobile

Mustard, Milk, and Gin • Megan Denton Ray

Dusk & Dust • Esteban Rodriguez

Rodeo in Reverse • Lindsey Alexander

Magic City Gospel • Ashley M. Jones

Wedding Pulls • J.K. Daniels

Punch • Ray McManus